W9-AUM-247

A More Perfect Union
The Story of Our Constitution

BY

BETSY AND GIULIO MAESTRO

LOTHROP, LEE & SHEPARD BOOKS
NEW YORK

GRATEFUL ACKNOWLEDGMENT is made to Dave Kimball and Anna Coxe Toogood, staff historians at Independence National Historical Park, Philadelphia, Pennsylvania, for checking the manuscript for accuracy.

First Edition 3 4 5 6 7 8 9 10

Library of Congress Cataloging in Publication Data
Maestro, Betsy. A more perfect union.
Summary: Describes how the Constitution was drafted and ratified.
1. United States. Constitutional Convention (1787)—Juvenile literature. 2. United States—Constitutional history—Juvenile literature. [1. United States. Constitutional Convention (1787) 2. United States. Constitutional history] I. Maestro, Giulio, ill.
II. Title. KF4520.Z9M33 1987 342.73'0292 87-4083
ISBN 0-688-06839-1 347.302292 ISBN 0-688-06840-5 (lib. bdg.)

Two hundred years ago, America was still a very young country. Representatives from the thirteen colonies met in 1776 to write the Declaration of Independence, which told King George III of England that the colonies wanted to rule themselves. The colonists formed their own government and fought the Revolutionary War to win their freedom.

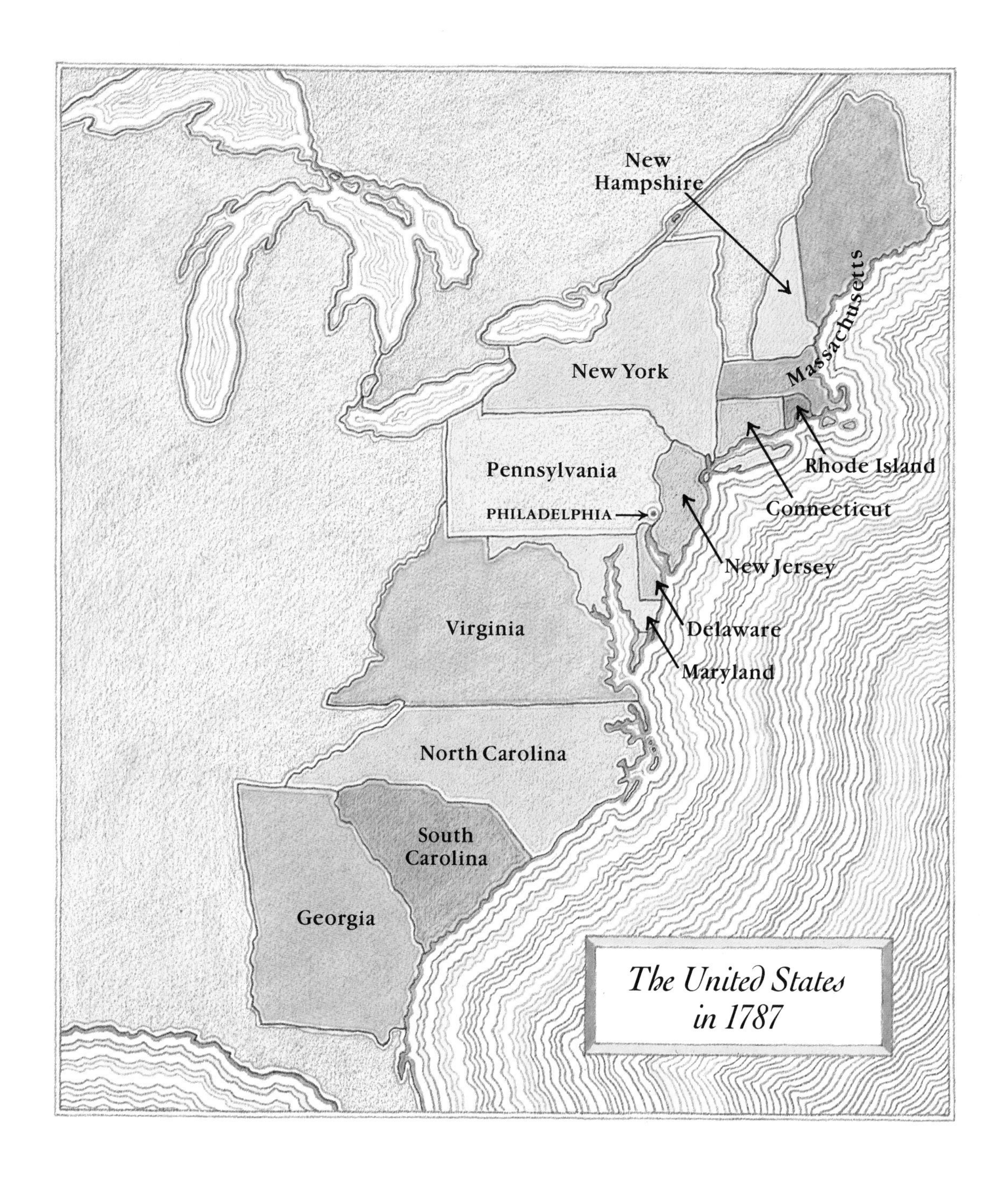

But ten years later, in 1786, America was in trouble. The government was not working well. Many people were poor. The thirteen states were not cooperating with one another. The government had no way to raise money, and there was no President to help the states work together as one nation.

The leaders of the new country were very worried and sad to see America in such trouble. They were afraid the country would fall apart if something was not done soon to make the government strong. These men decided to hold a special meeting, called a convention, to figure out what could be done. A few leaders from each state were invited to come to Philadelphia in May 1787.

Important men began arriving in Philadelphia. George Washington and James Madison came from Virginia. Alexander Hamilton was sent from New York, and Benjamin Franklin was there to speak for Pennsylvania. Many delegates stayed at the Indian Queen, one of the nicest inns.

Even before the convention began, the men were talking over their ideas and plans. Nearly all of them knew one another, as some of them had helped to write the Declaration of Independence, many had fought in the Revolutionary War, and most had served in the government. Now they were all anxious to help their country again.

The convention was to begin on May 14, but most of the delegates did not arrive by that date. Travel was very slow in those days. Some of the men came long distances by horseback, carriage, or ship.

The trip to Philadelphia from New Hampshire or Georgia could take two or three weeks. In addition, the weather was bad. Finally, by May 25, most of the delegates had arrived, and the convention began.

The convention took place in the State House on Chestnut Street. This building, which we now call Independence Hall, is where the Declaration of Independence had been signed eleven years before. At the very first meeting, the delegates voted to make George Washington the leader of the convention.

James Madison offered to write down everything that happened during the meetings, so there would be a record of all that was said and done. Even though the convention lasted for sixteen weeks, Madison did not miss a single meeting. His work was so important that he is called the Father of the Constitution.

When George Washington took his place at the desk on the platform, Benjamin Franklin noticed a sun carved on his chair. Franklin wondered whether it was a rising sun or a setting sun. He did not have much time to think about it, however, as the work of the convention had begun.

During the next few days, the men made a set of rules to help the convention run smoothly. Some of the rules were: each state would have one vote; a majority, or more than half the votes, would rule; and everything that happened at the meetings would be kept secret until after the convention was over.

Some of those who had arrived in Philadelphia early, including George Washington and James Madison, had come up with a plan to form a new government. Governor Edmund Randolph of Virginia presented this plan to the convention, so it became known as the Virginia Plan. The plan called for a government elected, or chosen, by the people. It would have three parts: a President, a congress or group of people to make laws, and a law court to make decisions about those laws.

Each state would choose delegates to serve in Congress. The number of delegates from each state would depend on the size of the state. This meant that big states would have more power than small states because they would have more votes in Congress.

Many of the delegates were very surprised by the Virginia Plan. They thought the convention would fix up the old government, not make a new one. They had to decide. Should they create a new government for America?

They took a vote and the yeses won. Now the job of the convention would be to write a constitution, a set of rules for forming a government, and another set of rules for the new government to follow.

Right away the delegates began to argue. The members from small states thought the Virginia Plan was unfair. They wanted each state to have the same number of representatives. Other delegates were afraid to let the people choose the President. They felt that ordinary citizens would make a bad choice. The delegates argued for weeks.

Finally, some members from the small states came up with a plan of their own called the New Jersey Plan. It said that, except for some small changes, the old government was fine. The most important thing the New Jersey Plan said was that all the states, no matter what their size, would have the same number of representatives.

After a few days of talking, the majority voted against the New Jersey Plan. The delegates from small states had lost their fight, and were bitterly disappointed, but they decided to work with the other delegates to come up with a plan that would satisfy both large and small states. By mid-July, with the help of some delegates from Connecticut, a compromise was worked out. Each

side had given up something it wanted in order to create a plan that both sides could accept. The plan was called the Great Compromise or the Connecticut Compromise. It was made up of some parts of the Virginia Plan, some parts of the New Jersey Plan, and some new ideas from both sides.

That summer in Philadelphia was hot, and the men were very tired. Most of them took some time now for a short vacation. They saw the sights of the city and enjoyed their free days. Some of them borrowed books from the library that Benjamin Franklin had started years before.

However, a small group of delegates called the Committee of Detail did not take a vacation. They gathered together all the parts of the new plan for the Constitution and wrote a first draft, or working copy. When the whole group of fifty-five delegates returned to the convention, they were able to look over this draft of the document that would govern all the American people.

On August 6, the delegates began to examine the draft of the new Constitution. Every sentence was argued, debated, and discussed by the members of the convention. By the end of the month, the delegates had agreed on almost everything. Again, the spirit of compromise saved the day.

Then another committee; the Committee of Style and Arrangement, went to work. Its members rewrote the final draft, making sure that every word was just right. At last, the Constitution was complete. Copies were printed and given to the delegates.

On September 15, the delegates voted to sign the new Constitution. Forty-two members were present, and only three did not agree to sign. Then the words were copied onto parchment, a very special kind of paper that lasts for a long time.

On Monday, September 17, 1787, the convention had its final meeting. Thirty-nine delegates signed the new Constitution. Some of the original fifty-five delegates had left the convention in anger because they did not approve of the new Constitution. Some others would have signed, but had to return home early.

The signing of the Constitution was a formal ceremony. George Washington was the first to write his name. Then the other thirty-eight men followed. Although it was a serious and important moment, it was also a very happy one.

Ben Franklin commented that at last he knew for sure what kind of sun was on Washington's chair—it was a rising sun! Everyone felt this was a good sign for the rising young country. Now all the men were anxious to get home. Many had not seen their families for months.

Much hard work still lay ahead. The Constitution had to be ratified, or approved, in each state before it could become law. The delegates had to convince the people in their home states to vote for the new Constitution.

Copies were sent to all the state governments. Each of the thirteen states would hold its own convention to vote. If nine of the thirteen states, or a two-thirds majority, voted for the new Constitution, the new government would be set up.

Many people were in favor of the new Constitution and many were against it. Those who didn't like it were afraid the new government would be too strong—that living in America would be much the same as living under English rule. The debates in the states went on, and in December 1787, Delaware became the

first state to approve the new Constitution. Pennsylvania, New Jersey, Georgia, and Connecticut quickly followed. Massachusetts came next in February 1788, after a very close vote in the state convention. By June, after Maryland and South Carolina had ratified, eight states had agreed to the new government.

HAMILTON

Now only one more state was needed for the new Constitution to become law. On June 21, 1788, New Hampshire voted yes. America would have a new government. The state of Virginia soon ratified as well.

When July 4 came, huge celebrations were held in many cities. In New York, a big ship was pulled through the streets in a parade. In Philadelphia, there was a parade made up of eighty-eight groups of marchers, some on floats.

New York State soon accepted the new Constitution. A date was set for the first election, by the people, of a President of the United States. George Washington was everyone's choice; he was elected by unanimous vote. On April 30, 1789, he took the oath of office, promising to serve his country well. Finally, by May 1790, all thirteen states had ratified the Constitution. Now the new nation truly could be called the United States of America.

A new Congress was elected, and it immediately went to work. Law courts were set up, and the new government seemed strong and sound.

But still some Americans worried. They believed that certain important rights of the people were not protected under the Constitution. So, to ease these fears, Congress proposed some additions to the Constitution.

The first ten additions, or amendments, are known as the Bill of Rights. In part, they state that people have the right to say what they want, go where they want, and pray to God in the way they want, without fear that the government will stop them. The Bill of Rights has turned out to be a very important part of the Constitution. It protects people from losing the freedom that is so much a part of American life.

Over the years, sixteen other amendments have been added. Our Constitution was written so that, as times change, it can change to meet the needs of our growing country.

Today, some two hundred years after it was written, the Constitution is still the basis of American government and the American people's way of life. It is the oldest written set of rules for running a country still in use in the world. It created a government that has worked better and longer than any other in history.

The Founding Fathers, as the authors of the Constitution are called, wrote the Constitution with the idea that the power of government should come from the people. This idea of each citizen playing a part in government is one of the principles that makes America strong. Power from the people, protected and guaranteed by the Constitution, has kept a union of states, now grown to fifty, together all these years.

THE CONSTITUTION OF THE UNITED STATES

PREAMBLE

We the People of the United States, in Order to form a more perfect Union, establish Justice, insure domestic Tranquility, provide for the common defence, promote the general Welfare, and secure the Blessings of Liberty to ourselves and our Posterity, do ordain and establish this Constitution for the United States of America.

SUMMARY OF THE ARTICLES OF THE CONSTITUTION

ARTICLE I

Lists rules for forming and running Congress, the law-making branch of government. Divides Congress into two houses, the Senate and the House of Representatives, and sets out the duties of each house. Lists the powers of the federal government.

ARTICLE II

Calls for a President to carry out the nation's laws. Describes procedures for electing the President and lists the President's powers.

ARTICLE III

Establishes a Supreme Court. Defines, and sets out laws for dealing with, treason against the United States.

ARTICLE IV

Forbids any state from treating a citizen of another state differently from its own citizens. Gives Congress the power to admit new states to the union.

ARTICLE V

Lists steps for amending (adding to or changing) the Constitution. Changes approved by at least three-fourths of the states become law.

ARTICLE VI

Makes the new Constitution the supreme law of the land, and requires all Federal and state officials to support it.

ARTICLE VII

Establishes that if at least nine states ratify the Constitution of 1787, it is considered the law of the land.

The United States Constitution is on permanent display at the National Archives in Washington, D.C.

SIGNERS OF THE CONSTITUTION

The names of the delegates appear as they actually wrote them, and in the order they were signed.

Go. Washington—Presidt.
and deputy from Virginia.
[*George Washington*]

NEW HAMPSHIRE
John Langdon
Nicholas Gilman

MASSACHUSETTS
Nathaniel Gorham
Rufus King

CONNECTICUT
Wm. Saml. Johnson
[*William Samuel Johnson*]
Roger Sherman

NEW YORK
Alexander Hamilton

NEW JERSEY
Wil: Livingston [*William Livingston*]
David Brearley.
Wm. Paterson. [*William Paterson*]
Jona: Dayton [*Jonathan Dayton*]

PENNSYLVANIA
B Franklin [*Benjamin Franklin*]
Thomas Mifflin
Robt Morris [*Robert Morris*]
Geo. Clymer [*George Clymer*]
Thos. FitzSimons [*Thomas Fitzsimons*]
Jared Ingersoll
James Wilson
Gouv Morris [*Gouverneur Morris*]

DELAWARE
Geo: Read [*George Read*]
Gunning Bedford jun
John Dickinson
Richard Bassett
Jaco: Broom [*Jacob Broom*]

MARYLAND
James McHenry
Dan of St. Thos. Jenifer
[*Daniel of St. Thomas Jenifer*]
Danl. Carroll. [*Daniel Carroll*]

VIRGINIA
John Blair—
James Madison Jr.

NORTH CAROLINA
Wm. Blount [*William Blount*]
Richd. Dobbs Spaight. [*Richard Dobbs Spaight*]
Hu Williamson [*Hugh Williamson*]

SOUTH CAROLINA
J. Rutledge [*John Rutledge*]
Charles Cotesworth Pinckney
Charles Pinckney
Pierce Butler.

GEORGIA
William Few
Abr Baldwin [*Abraham Baldwin*]

Other Delegates to the Constitutional Convention: Elbridge Gerry, Caleb Strong (MA) • Oliver Ellsworth (CT) • John Lansing, Robert Yates (NY) • William C. Houston (NJ) • Luther Martin, John Francis Mercer (MD) • James McClurg, George Mason, Edmund Randolph, George Wythe (VA) • William R. Davie, Alexander Martin (NC) • William Houstoun, William Pierce (GA)

TABLE OF DATES

1774 The First Continental Congress, a committee of colonists, meets to consider taking action against unfair British rule. Writes and adopts a Declaration of Rights for the colonies.

1775 American Revolution begins with fighting at Lexington and Concord, Massachusetts. First meeting of the Second Continental Congress.

1776 Declaration of Independence from Britain is adopted by the Second Continental Congress.

1777 Second Continental Congress creates the Articles of Confederation, a set of laws for governing the new states.

1781 Articles of Confederation become the law of the land. Last battle of the Revolution ends at Yorktown, Virginia, when British surrender to General George Washington.

1783 United States and Britain sign Treaty of Paris to end the American Revolution.

1785 Disputes arise between the thirteen states.

1786 Convention is held in Annapolis, Maryland, to discuss problems between the states. Delegates plan a convention of the states in Philadelphia, Pennsylvania.

1787 Delegates to the Philadelphia convention write the United States Constitution to replace the Articles of Confederation. Constitution is signed in September and ratified by three states by December.

1788 Constitution is ratified by six more states and becomes law on June 21.

1789 George Washington is elected first President of the United States. Bill of Rights is written.

1791 Virginia is the eleventh state to approve the Bill of Rights, making it part of the Constitution.

NOTES ON THE CONNECTICUT COMPROMISE

Delegates from small states objected to the Virginia Plan because it called for more congressional representatives from large states than from small states. The members from small states wanted each state to have the same number of representatives in the government so that all the states would have equal power.

Delegates from large states objected to the New Jersey Plan because they did not think all the people would be represented fairly if each state had an equal number of representatives in Congress, regardless of the size of the state's population.

William Samuel Johnson, Roger Sherman, and Oliver Ellsworth, the delegates from Connecticut, helped lead the way to a compromise that was fair to all the states. Called the Connecticut Compromise or the Great Compromise, the plan divided Congress into two houses: an Upper House, called the Senate, to which each state would send two senators chosen by its state legislature; and a Lower House, called the House of Representatives, where the number of delegates from each state would be determined by the population; these delegates would be elected by the people. A state's population was held to be the number of free men plus three-fifths of its slaves. Later amendments to the Constitution abolished slavery, and gave every adult, regardless of race or sex, the right to vote.

INTERESTING FACTS ABOUT THE CONVENTION AND THE DELEGATES

The average age of the delegates was forty-three. Benjamin Franklin, at eighty-one, was the oldest. Jonathan Dayton, the youngest, was twenty-six.

Twenty-one delegates had fought in the Revolutionary War, eight had signed the Declaration of Independence, and seven were or had been governors of their states.

Gouverneur Morris, James Wilson, James Madison, and Roger Sherman spoke more often than anyone else at the convention.

Delegates who argued for a strong central government included James Wilson, Charles C. Pinckney, and Gouverneur Morris. William Paterson, John Dickinson, and Luther Martin sided with those in favor of individual and states' rights.

The Committee of Detail wrote a rough first draft of the Constitution. John Rutledge, Edmund Randolph, Nathaniel Gorham, Oliver Ellsworth, and James Wilson served on this committee.

The Committee of Style and Arrangement polished the first draft, putting the wording into its final form. The committee members were Gouverneur Morris, Alexander Hamilton, Rufus King, William Samuel Johnson, and James Madison.

New Hampshire could not afford to advance expense money to its delegates. In late June, John Langdon and Nicholas Gilman decided to go to the convention anyway. They didn't reach Philadelphia until late July, when most of the debates were over.

George Mason, Edmund Randolph, and Elbridge Gerry voted against the Constitution and refused to sign it. If a bill of rights had been included, they might have signed.

Rhode Island sent no delegates to the convention and so had no signers.

ORDER AND DATES OF RATIFICATION OF THE CONSTITUTION

Delaware • December 7, 1787

Pennsylvania • December 12, 1787

New Jersey • December 18, 1787

Georgia • January 2, 1788

Connecticut • January 9, 1788

Massachusetts • February 6, 1788

Maryland • April 28, 1788

South Carolina • May 23, 1788

New Hampshire • June 21, 1788

Virginia • June 25, 1788

New York • July 26, 1788

North Carolina • November 21, 1789

Rhode Island • May 29, 1790

SUMMARY OF THE AMENDMENTS TO THE CONSTITUTION

The first ten amendments make up the Bill of Rights, adopted in 1791.

Amendment I Guarantees freedom of religion, of speech, and of the press. Gives the people the right to meet peaceably and the right to voice complaints to the government.

Amendment II Guarantees the right to keep and bear arms.

Amendment III Sets conditions for housing soldiers in peacetime and in wartime.

Amendment IV Guarantees the right to privacy. Limits the power of government to search and seize property.

Amendment V Establishes trial procedures. Forbids punishment without a trial. Guarantees compensation if property is taken by the government for public use.

Amendment VI Guarantees the right to a speedy, fair trial by jury in criminal cases.

Amendment VII Provides for a jury trial in civil lawsuits exceeding the value of twenty dollars.

Amendment VIII Prohibits excessive bail and fines, and cruel and unusual punishment.

Amendment IX The people hold more rights than only those listed in the Constitution.

Amendment X Powers not given by the Constitution to the central government, or forbidden to the states, are reserved for the states or the people.

XI (1798) Keeps any one of the states from being sued by citizens of another state or of a foreign country.

XII (1804) Sets presidential election procedures.

XIII (1865) Abolishes slavery.

XIV (1868) Forbids laws that unfairly deny citizens' rights and guarantees equal protection under the law to all.

XV (1870) Forbids depriving citizens of the right to vote because of their race or color.

XVI (1913) Authorizes an income tax.

XVII (1913) Calls for senators to be elected by direct vote of the people.

XVIII (1919) The Prohibition Amendment. Forbids the manufacture or sale of liquor.

XIX (1920) Grants women the right to vote.

XX (1933) Starts presidential and congressional terms in January.

XXI (1933) Repeals the Eighteenth Amendment.

XXII (1951) Bars any President from serving more than two terms (eight years).

XXIII (1961) Gives residents of the District of Columbia (Washington, D.C.) the right to vote for President.

XXIV (1964) Outlaws the payment of taxes as a voting requirement.

XXV (1967) Sets up rules for succession if a President cannot complete the term.

XXVI (1971) Lowers the legal voting age to eighteen.